DATE DUE

7/29			
GAYLORD			PRINTED IN U.S.A.

NEW ARTS & CRAFTS HOUSES

NEW ARTS & CRAFTS HOUSES

NEILL HEATH

NEW ARTS & CRAFTS HOUSES
Copyright 2005 © by COLLINS DESIGN and GRAYSON PUBLISHING, LLC

Full title page photograph by Robert Benson

HarperCollins books may be purchased for educational, business, or sales promotional use. For information, please write: Special Markets Department, HarperCollins Publishers Inc., 10 East 53rd Street, New York, NY 10022.

First Edition

First published in 2005 by:
Collins Design
An Imprint of HarperCollins*Publishers*
10 East 53rd Street
New York, NY 10022
Tel: (212) 207-7000
Fax: (212) 207-7654
collinsdesign@harpercollins.com
www.harpercollins.com

Distributed throughout the world by:
HarperCollins *Publishers*
10 East 53rd Street
New York, NY 10022
Fax: (212) 207-7654

Packaged by:
Grayson Publishing, LLC
James G. Trulove, Publisher
1250 28th Street NW
Washington, DC 20007
202-337-1380
jtrulove@aol.com
Graphic Design by: Agnieszka Stachowizc
Library of Congress Control Number: 2005931351

ISBN 10: 0-06-083334-3
ISBN 13: 978-0-06-083334-3
Manufactured in China
First printing, 2005
1 2 3 4 5 6 7 8 9 / 06 05 04 03

CONTENTS

FOREWORD

As a movement, Arts & Crafts never produced a strictly defined style in architecture or design. After all, it was originally an ideology that evolved as a movement in Britain around 1880 in response to a growing disenchantment among architects, artists, and craftsmen with industrialization and the impersonality of the machine age. Instead, the Arts & Crafts movement advocated the importance of individuality, simplicity, and the unity of handicraft and design. It also embraced nostalgia for rural traditions and regional styles and urged closeness to nature.

In Britain, architects and designers often looked to simple medieval forms as well as traditional rural or folk architecture—cottages, farmhouses, and country homes—frequently incorporating strong national or regional references.

Arts & Crafts crossed the Atlantic to the United States, where the style flourished in neighborhoods along the East Coast, in the Midwest, and on the West Coast, especially in California, Oregon, and Washington. Resort towns like Asheville, North Carolina, and communities like the Byrdcliffe Arts Colony in Woodstock, New York also embraced the Arts & Crafts style. Though the classic bungalow and cottage styles were most often seen, the sources were varied, ranging from European and Japanese forms to Colonial Revival and California Mission. Taking America's varied landscapes and climates into consideration, many architects and proponents also sought to reflect regional characteristics and use local materials and trades.

Then as now, most of the houses that best represent the Arts & Crafts aesthetic rely on simplicity to create more complex forms and stress the decorative properties inherent in construction. Houses are typically straightforward, defined by horizontal lines, and often characterized by overhanging eaves with braces, exposed rafter tails, and broad, solid chimneys. Natural materials—frequently from local sources—are used and include wooden shingles and siding or rough stucco, and beam timber post construction, and stone in all forms and shapes. Reflecting the Arts & Crafts interest in nature, a connection to the outdoors is expressed through broad covered porches, projecting balconies, terraces, and pergolas.

Where Victorian homes had formal plans with individual rooms for separate purposes, Arts & Crafts houses adopted a more modern plan to convey a feeling of spaciousness, even in smaller homes. Interiors were opened up, making it possible to see through one room to another, and often to the outdoors through doors or windows. To define space while retaining the openness, partial walls, simple columns, built-in bookcases or cabinets and spindled screens were used. Recesses and inglenooks created rooms within rooms. The interior palette was simple: wood, stone, tile, and plaster. Construction details like ceiling beams—exposed and emphasized—provided decoration, as applied ornament was nonexistent or rarely used. Of course, central to most Arts & Crafts homes were the living room and hearth, the *heart* of the house. In almost every house of this design, a prominent, solid fireplace is used to anchor the room and create a gathering place for family and friends.

Overall, as architectural historian Robert Winter notes in the following essay, from the Arts & Crafts viewpoint, a house was more than a roof overhead; it was a home, a sanctuary for the family. This is just as true today as it was 100 years ago, and the fully modern, Arts & Crafts—inspired homes in this book reflect this same concern with simplicity of style and respect for crafted details.

LEFT: *Wood characterizes Arts & Crafts houses and creates a sense of warmth and intimacy as demonstrated here in the Craftsman House in Menlo Park, California, by architect John Malick. Photograph by John Grove*

THE ARTS & CRAFTS STYLE

BY ROBERT WINTER

Not long ago my photographer, Alex Vertikoff, and I published a book that we called *Craftsman Style* (Abrams, 2004). The reviews were mostly positive, except that a critic for the National Trust's journal, *Preservation*, was disturbed that we had included a short section on the revival of the Arts & Crafts movement in recent years: "It is a pity that their book claims for it just a bit more scope and a longer duration than it deserves," he wrote condescendingly. "Where has this guy been?" I thought. True, he lives in Sonoma, California, which is off the beaten track, but he should have noticed the variations on the woodsy style of the early twentieth century that are being built in northern California as well as southern California and, indeed, all over the country, a phenomenon of considerable significance even though it was, in the past as it is in the present, by no means the predominant style in America.

William Morris (1834–1896), the English father of the Arts & Crafts (or Craftsman, in America) movement would be puzzled by the present interpretation of his ideas. Although trained as an architect, he was never very clear about the kind of architecture that he thought appropriate for his time, but the "Red House," designed by his friend Philip Webb for the Morrises and built on the southern edge of London in 1859, gives a suggestion of his ideal. The style of the house was based on that of the sixteenth- and seventeenth-century English

rural dwellings built for country squires and their likes, adequate in size but unpretentious in expression. It came as close to the spirit of Morris's beloved Middle Ages as he could get and still have all the necessary facilities for modern (nineteenth-century) living. It was (and is) a very beautiful building, with its high-pitched gables, asymmetrical plan, and lovely pink brick walls. It is the embodiment of Morris's idea of the simple but elegant home.

Morris had many friends who were architects, and all of them built in the style that he and Philip Webb had arrived at. They called it "Old English." Many architects outside Morris's circle also adopted this style, and it came to be the British mode of Arts & Crafts architecture. American architects such as Frank Lloyd Wright, Bernard Maybeck, and Charles and Henry Greene, who were to become the leaders of the American Arts & Crafts movement in architecture, knew the work of some members of the English school. C.F.A. Voysey, M.H. Baillie Scott, and the firm of Barry Parker and Raymond Unwin had been published in American periodicals. But by and large the Americans avoided the Old English style and instead latched on to another English mode—Richard Norman Shaw's Queen Anne.

Shaw also designed in the English vernacular of the sixteenth and seventeenth centuries, but instead of using stucco on the exterior surfaces of his houses, he covered them with red brick and flat, red

tiles. American architects such as H.H. Richardson and McKim, Mead and White picked up on Shaw's manner but substituted American shingles for English tiles, creating what the Yale architectural historian Vincent Scully Jr. has called the "Shingle style." This nineteenth-century development was the basis for the early-twentieth-century American Craftsman style.

About 1900, three other stylistic modes were mixed with the Shingle style in order to give it even more interest—the Japanese temple, the Swiss chalet, and the Tudor house. In good hands this amalgam came out well. Details from all these styles gave additional picturesqueness to the original Shingle style. The congeries had in common not only a wooden structure but also exposed wood on their exterior walls. With their horizontal lines they helped fit the house into its natural environment.

Architects saw their creations as consequences of "building with nature." Again, William Morris would not have understood that the American Craftsman style came directly out of his call for simplicity and harmony with nature—indeed, that the Americans, of whom he was not overly fond, were actually designing the quiet, nonassertive architecture that he suggested in his own house and in his novel *News from Nowhere* (1890), whose subtitle, after all, was *An Epoch of Rest.*

At the beginning of this essay I mentioned my observation that the Arts & Crafts architecture of the early twentieth century was, after a period of ridicule and neglect, coming back and that its revival has considerable significance. Of course, it is now a style that can be applied and manipulated, so that it has lost some of the social meaning that it had in its first flowering. Yet as the pages that follow demonstrate, it has retained characteristics that minister to the present state of civilization, some of them found in the original Old English style. It is quiet and self-effacing, fading into nature rather than competing with it as Victorian building and modernist ones do. In a society of growing complexity, it is also a relief from the hurly-burly of the present. Its usually dark interiors rest the eyes. The fire in the fireplace is still better at expressing the heart of the house than the television set that often stands beside it. It's not just a house, it's home.

Robert Winter is the Arthur G. Coons Professor of the History of Ideas, Emeritus, at Occidental College in Los Angeles. He is a well-known author and lecturer on the Arts & Crafts movement in the United States and has written numerous books on the subject, including his most recent Craftsman Style, *as well as* The California Bungalow. *He is the editor of* Toward a Simpler Way of Life: The Arts and Crafts Architects of California. *Winter lives in a historic Pasadena bungalow.*

NANCEKIVELL HOUSE

The design of this house, on a sloping lot in a suburb of the Twin Cities, reflects a strong response to the landscape and includes many updated Craftsman details. With many mature trees, natural light was limited and the predominant views were to the west, down the hill. The rooms are arranged as if along a path descending the hill, responding to the grade while at the same time taking advantage of the view and seasonal light. According to the architect, when one walks through the house, one still feels the presence of the hill.

To help define a scheme for the design, the owners presented the architect with a collection of pictures and photos from other houses that included elements and features they admired, notably shingle- and prairie-style houses, trellises, entry courtyards, and walls of stone, wood, and brick. Drawn to color, form, and detail, the owners also wanted a comfortable family home with spaces that would allow for both privacy and togetherness.

All these considerations were incorporated into a house where the public and private areas are separated by these gradual changes in elevation. The living room, dining room, and kitchen are spatially open to one another, but clearly separated areas—linked by the glass entryway—were created for the adults on the second floor of the main long section and their two teenage children in a side wing.

Dining, kitchen, and living areas extend in a single, open, linear sequence, each space a few steps down from the other. Within this long open space, maple cabinetry partitions serve as partial walls that provide definition and a sense of enclosure for the spaces.

ARCHITECT **SALA ARCHITECTS, INC.**
PHOTOGRAPHER **GEORGE HEINRICH**
LOCATION **TWIN CITIES, MINNESOTA**

The master bedroom is above, tucked into the rooflines of the main south-facing gable, opening out to a balcony perched over the courtyard.

A large trellised courtyard flanks the house on the gabled side, acting as an exterior entryway and a link between the central form and the side wing. This long main section of the house has a shallow depth, which permits the winter sun to flow into the house. Deep overhangs and a balcony over the courtyard shade the house in summer.

PREVIOUS PAGES: *True to Arts & Crafts design, this house blurs the division between the exterior and the interior. This house follows the landscape, with rooms arranged as if along a path descending the hill, taking advantage of the view and the changing seasons.*

UPPER LEVEL/LOWER LEVEL

MAIN LEVEL

SECTION

SITE PLAN

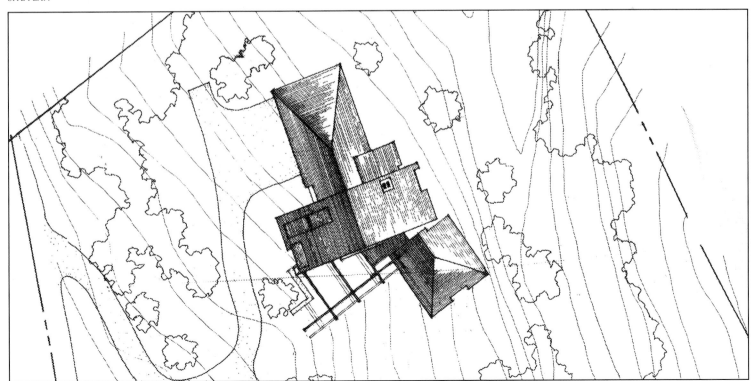

LEFT: *A large trellised courtyard spans the gabled side of the house, serving as an exterior entryway and a link between the outside garden, the main house, and the side wing. In summer, deep overhangs shade the house; in winter, the sun flows into the long and shallow main house.*

RIGHT: *A large stone chimney and fine wood millwork underscore the craftsmanship with which the house was built.*

LEFT: *The dining area collects natural light from a series of clerestory windows.*

RIGHT: *Breakfast nook in the kitchen.*

ABOVE: *The dining, kitchen, and living areas follow an open, linear sequence. Definition and a sense of enclosure is created by cabinetry partitions that serve as partial walls.*

LEFT: *Staircase detail*

RIGHT: *Broad beams emphasize the importance of structure and construction. The second-floor master bedroom in the main gable opens out to a private balcony perched over the courtyard.*

GERVAIS HOUSE

An undistinguished spec house in a desirable Seattle neighborhood was dramatically transformed by the architect and owners into a contemporary interpretation of a Seattle bungalow. Located around the corner from a waterfront park, the original house was a late-1960s, two-story structure with small rooms and a cramped layout. A dark foyer led to a living room on the left, and on the right, a dining room, half bath, and dated kitchen. Upstairs, three bedrooms shared a single bath in the hall; the fourth, master bedroom, had a small attached bath.

The decision was made to extensively rework the 1,900- square-foot house rather than completely demolish it. While the original structure was largely gutted, the framing was kept in place and the 1960s footprint remains within the new house. The floor plan was opened up to create a more inviting, free flow between rooms, and a 2,000-square-foot addition was added.

Working with the original building, one challenge was to reflect the mass and detailing of the Arts & Crafts style. Dormers were added to define the house and provide articulation. The windows were replaced and, in many cases, reconfigured in the design. Classic bungalow details were used on the exterior, including broad eaves, exposed rafter tails, and trellises. A covered front porch with battered columns atop stone piers creates a dramatic entryway to the house.

Inside, the layout was reconfigured to create an open interior plan. New windows and skylights bring natural light into all sections of the house. Half walls with battered columns separate the living and dining rooms, both of which look onto the front porch through large bay windows. The living room has a wooden fireplace mantle stained black, set with dark iridescent tiles.

ARCHITECT WAI/GORNY INC.
PHOTOGRAPHER RICHARD MCNAMEE
LOCATION SEATTLE, WASHINGTON

Throughout the house Craftsman-inspired details are used, including wainscoting, crown molding, and wood door casings. In the dining room, a coffered ceiling lends interest. Flooring was replaced with wide-plank oak in the living and dining areas.

An addition included a new family room, painting studio, home office, laundry room, two bedrooms, and childrens' playroom. Above the garage, a loft space was refinished as a separate den or apartment.

PREVIOUS PAGES: *An extensive renovation transformed a nondescript house into an updated version of a classic Seattle bungalow.*

SECOND-FLOOR PLAN

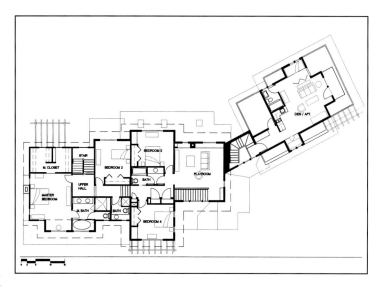

FIRST-FLOOR PLAN

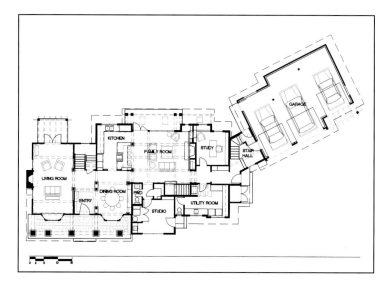

LEFT: *The original house was built in the late 1960s.*

ABOVE AND ABOVE RIGHT: *A covered front porch with battered columns atop stone piers creates a dramatic entryway to the house.*

LEFT: *The house was extensively remodeled rather than demolished, and the 1960s footprint remains. The floor plan was reworked to create open, more usable spaces and many Arts & Crafts details were added.*

ABOVE: *The living room details include a wooden fireplace mantle stained black, set with dark iridescent tiles.*

ABOVE: *The family room, with beamed ceiling and paneled fireplace surround. A wall of windows and French doors provides a link to the outside and the rear patio.*

LEFT: *The kitchen is open to the family room. The cabinets are tansu-inspired in mahogany. Honed granite was used for the countertops.*

RIGHT: *The rear patio is an outdoor living room. Craftsman details on the rear of the house include broad eaves and exposed rafter tails.*

CRAFTSMAN HOUSE

For clients who admired the classic California Arts & Crafts houses found throughout the San Francisco Bay Area, architect John Malick designed this richly detailed Craftsman house in Menlo Park. This large, comfortable home is well suited for a young family, combining four bedrooms, four baths, home offices for both parents, living room, dining room, kitchen open to both family room and breakfast area, laundry, mudroom, and a small playroom.

The home is developed around a central stair hall with high clerestory windows that naturally ventilate the house. A formal living room and a dining room flank the front portion of the entry hall.

The rear area of the home is devoted to the family, with a large family room and open kitchen separated by an island. The kitchen complements the period architecture, with traditional plumbing fixtures, paneled appliances, and stone countertops. Numerous double-hung windows bring light into the house and French doors open to a rear porch with a trellis.

The large rear porch and outdoor eating area face the rear garden with a grove of mature redwoods. An outdoor fieldstone fireplace makes sitting outside in the evenings comfortable despite northern California's cool climate. The upstairs bedrooms open to covered sleeping porches, similar to California homes from the early 1900s, and views of the redwoods.

Natural materials and varied Craftsman detail are incorporated throughout the house. Simple vertical-grain Douglas fir paneling is used throughout the interior of the house and, along with casework and beamed ceilings, develops the warm, casual

---

ARCHITECT JOHN MALICK AND ASSOCIATES
PHOTOGRAPHER JOHN GROVE
LOCATION MENLO PARK, CALIFORNIA

character that the clients sought. Special interior details include custom-designed bronze hardware, air grilles, lighting fixtures, and fireplace doors fabricated from copper to further enhance the Arts & Crafts character of the home.

PREVIOUS PAGES: *This finely detailed Craftsman house in Menlo Park integrates many design aspects, including specially fabricated lighting fixtures, bronze hardware, air grilles, and fireplace doors.*

SECOND-FLOOR PLAN

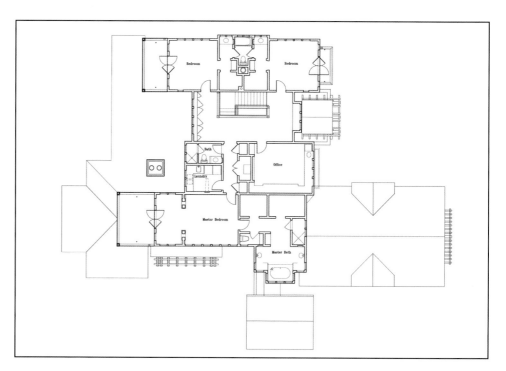

FIRST-FLOOR PLAN

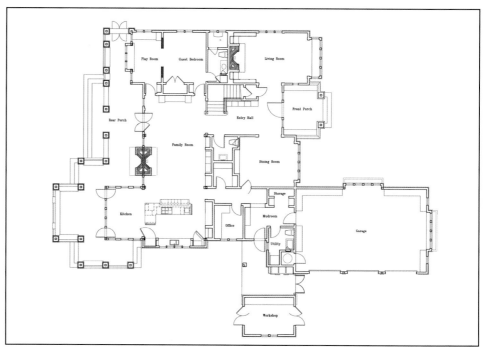

EAST ELEVATION

REAR ELEVATION

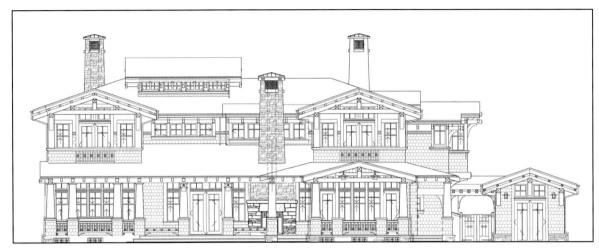

FRONT ELEVATION

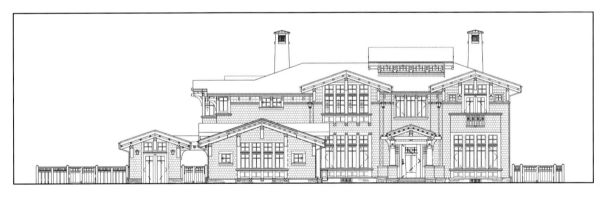

WEST ELEVATION

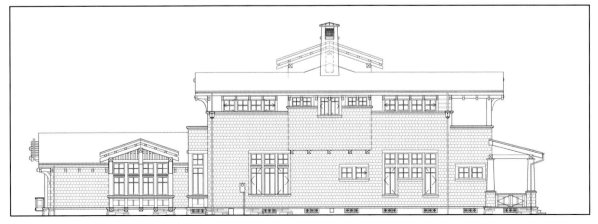

LEFT: *The large rear porch and outdoor dining area facing the rear garden and redwood grove blur the line between interior and exterior. An outdoor fieldstone fireplace makes sitting outside in the evenings comfortable despite the cool northern California climate.*

ABOVE: *The upstairs bedrooms open to covered sleeping porches, similar to California homes from the early 1900s, and views of the redwoods.*

LEFT AND ABOVE: *The central hall features board and batten paneling, a built-in hall bench, and a beamed ceiling. Vertical-grain Douglas fir is used throughout the interior of the house and conveys a warm, intimate quality.*

ABOVE: *The large family room and open kitchen in the rear of the house are centered on the fieldstone fireplace, the heart of the Arts & Crafts home, The open kitchen is separated from the living area by cabinetry.*

RIGHT: *The kitchen complements the period architecture, with traditional plumbing fixtures, paneled appliances, and stone countertops.*

ABOVE: *The living room features built-in bookcases and trim in Douglas fir. The fireplace has an overmantel with brackets and board and batten paneling.*

LEFT: *The large bay window in the living room, with its cushioned window seats, provides a comfortable recess, an intimate retreat from the larger room.*

ABOVE LEFT AND ABOVE:
*Home offices provide private retreats
for both parents.*

LEFT: *Special interior details include
custom-designed lighting fixtures as well
as bronze hardware, air grilles, and
fireplace doors.*

ABOVE: *Reflecting the view that outdoor sleeping provided healthful benefits, sleeping porches were popular at the close of the nineteenth century. The master bedroom opens onto a covered sleeping porch and views of the redwood grove.*

RIGHT: *Master bathroom recalls period architecture and features traditional plumbing fixtures and stone countertops.*

WEBB-COVE HOUSE

Nestled on a mountainside just outside of Asheville, North Carolina, this house combines Craftsman features with an open layout and high ceilings that suggest a more spacious house. Its modest footprint and simple form blend well with the surrounding wooded landscape.

Though private, the 5-acre site is on a slope and the southern exposure faces uphill. Bringing sunlight into the house therefore was a prime consideration in the orientation of the house. In addition, tall windows on the two upper levels allow for an abundance of daylight.

The clients had owned an Arts & Crafts bungalow in Atlanta and asked the architect to design the new house with those features. On the exterior, projecting roof beams, board and batten siding, and cedar shingles add textural interest. The front entrance porch features a post and beam roof supported by wooden posts atop stone piers and a flagstone floor.

Inside, the cross-gable plan works well, minimizing circulation, with all spaces connecting from a central entry hall, which also doubles as an open gallery. To take advantage of seasonally changing views across the mountains, the living room is situated at the back of the house. A large outdoor porch, covered to provide shade in summer, is accessed through a glass door in the living room and another in the kitchen. The kitchen and dining room are open to one another, and French doors lead from the dining room to a stone terrace outside. A guest bedroom lies off the gallery. Upstairs are the master bedroom and bath, as well as a private den and home office.

ARCHITECT **SAMSEL ARCHITECTS**
PHOTOGRAPHER **SAMSEL ARCHITECTS**
LOCATION **ASHEVILLE, NORTH CAROLINA**

BASEMENT PLAN

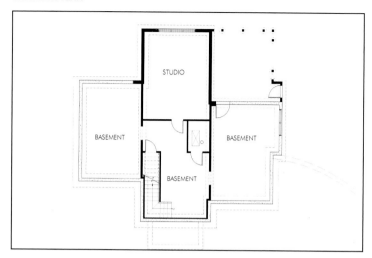

FIRST-FLOOR PLAN

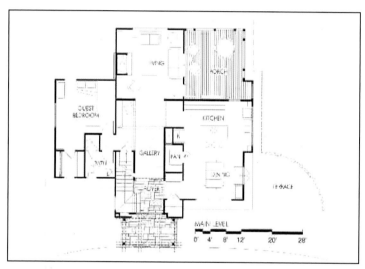

SECOND-FLOOR PLAN

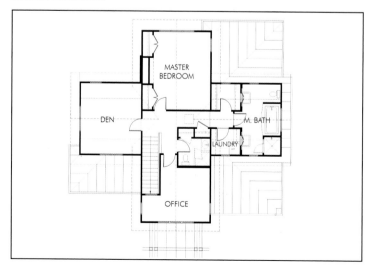

PREVIOUS PAGES: *This house echoes the rustic and picturesque Arts & Crafts and Shingle styles widely built in the Asheville area at the turn of the century. The house combines an open layout and high ceilings that suggest a more spacious dwelling.*

RIGHT: *The front entrance porch features a post and beam roof supported by wooden posts atop stone piers. Board and batten siding and cedar shingles add textural interest.*

LEFT: *Simple interior details and finishes combine well in this house. Stained pine trim was used extensively throughout the house.*

RIGHT: *Inside, the first-floor plan is open, with all spaces connecting from a central gallery.*

ABOVE: *Light walls and dark wood trim characterize this house. Here, the fireplace is made with rough-cut stone from the area.*

TOP RIGHT AND RIGHT: *The kitchen is open to the dining room. French doors lead from the dining room to a stone terrace on the side of the house.*

LEFT: *Kitchen*

RIGHT: *A large, covered outdoor porch on the rear of the house serves as a shaded retreat in the summer.*

MT. BAKER HOUSE

This new house was built as the first of five speculative houses in a small, planned development in Seattle's historic Mt. Baker neighborhood. The goal was to create five complementary but distinctive homes—most designed by architects—that blended into a well-established residential environment. The surrounding neighborhood is a veritable catalog of the styles that have influenced Seattle residential architecture over the past 100 years, including many classic Craftsman houses and other styles. Some of Seattle's most famous and prestigious architects are represented in Mt. Baker. Owing to a shared sense of scale and relationship to the street, as well as mature gardens that lend texture and cohesiveness to the neighborhood, the community gracefully accommodates the range of architectural styles.

Borrowing from the Craftsman tradition while expressing a more contemporary aesthetic, this modern house respects the attributes that define this neighborhood. Materials such as hard panel, aluminum windows, steel and fir handrails, as well as modern lighting and vivid colors bring the house unequivocally into the present; but the attention to detail, the expression of separate materials, and the clarity of the construction reflect the Craftsman roots.

Special attention was given to the landscape and the interplay between the exterior colors and the plantings. The signature evergreen in front of the house is a classic Craftsman touch that lends a sense of permanence and age to a new house

The first-floor layout is linear in that the service areas, including baths, small study area, and kitchen, lie to the right of the house, while the living room, dining room, and family room lie to the left.

ARCHITECT **JOHNSTON ARCHITECTS**
PHOTOGRAPHER **MICHAEL MOORE**
LOCATION **SEATTLE, WASHINGTON**

The living room and the dining room are separated by a partial wall. This lends the house the sense of a great room, but at the same time suggests more formal, separate spaces. In the living room, the fireplace is a pared-down, slightly tapered brick version of those often seen in Craftsman-era homes. Cherry floors lend a rich, warm feeling to the house.

The kitchen opens onto the family room with doors to a covered exterior porch on the side of the house.

Upstairs, three bedrooms and two full baths are located off a central hall. From the master bedroom overlooking the rear of the house, French doors lead to a small private balcony.

PREVIOUS PAGES: *This house was designed to blend into a well-established residential neighborhood that contained numerous classic Craftsman homes from the early twentieth century.*

SECOND FLOOR

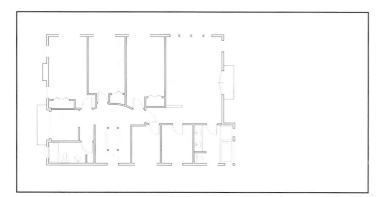

FIRST FLOOR

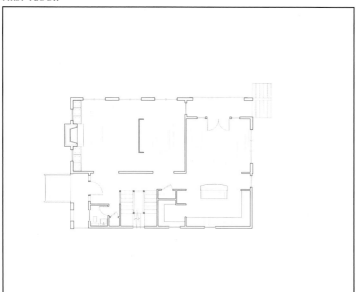

FOUNDATION PLAN

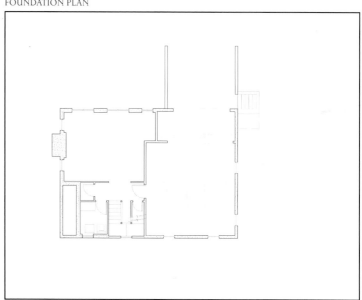

NORTH ELEVATION

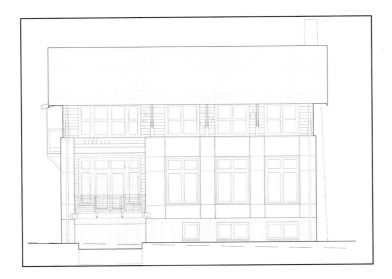

SOUTH ELEVATION

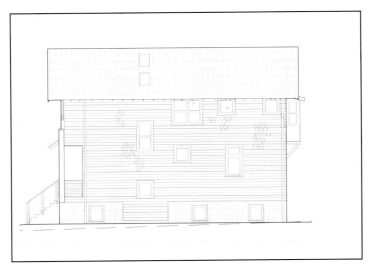

EAST ELEVATION

WEST ELEVATION

ABOVE AND LEFT: *Contemporary materials such as hard panel, aluminum windows, and steel and fir handrails were used on the exterior.*

RIGHT: *Borrowing from the Craftsman tradition while expressing a more contemporary aesthetic, this modern house respects the attributes that define this neighborhood.*

LEFT: *While modern lighting and vivid colors are used with this house, the attention to detail, the expression of separate materials, and the clarity of the construction reflect the Craftsman roots.*

RIGHT: *The focus of this living room is the fireplace, an updated, slightly tapered brick version of those often seen in Seattle's Craftsman-era homes.*

ABOVE LEFT AND LEFT: *The living room and the dining room are separated by a partial wall. The spaciousness and flow of a great room is maintained, but the sense is created of more formal, separate spaces.*

ABOVE: *The family room with doors to a covered exterior porch on the side of the house.*

RIGHT: *The kitchen*

LAKE HOUSE

This cottage sits on one of the thousands of lakes that dot the Northwoods of Wisconsin. Heavily wooded with mature pine and spruce, the lakefront site affords the owners privacy even though the total acreage of the lot is small. The back elevation of the lot drops down to the shoreline, creating open views from the house across the water. To take full advantage of the view, the house is positioned so that the main rooms and bedrooms all face the lake.

The owners are attracted to turn-of-the-century German folk and cottage styles, so a steeply pitched roof was important in the design of the new house. The result is a roof that defines this house. Massive and steeply pitched, the roof creates a silhouette and establishes the house's personality, unifying a combination of exterior features. Exterior clapboard, sawn-shingle siding and vertical beams lend an interesting irregularity to the exterior surface and add warmth to the house. The dense stucco-over-concrete foundation, flared from the base to the start of the clapboard, suggests strength, a house rooted to the site.

Inside, the layout of the house is simple and straightforward, with defined informal family rooms and more formal public spaces. From the entrance foyer inside, views extend through the dining and living areas to the lake.

The interior Arts & Crafts influences first become apparent in the entryway. A low, built-in hall bench forms part of the stairwell. The stairwell itself is defined by an open screen of spindles that extend from the back of the hall bench to a band of horizontal trim.

The living and dining rooms are connected through a large doorway framed by low walls on each side. The careful alignment of ceiling beams helps define the space and provides a sense of enclosure. At the center of the living room is a large fireplace, finished in the same rough stucco used on the exterior foundation. Situated beneath the beams overhead and

---

ARCHITECT SALA ARCHITECTS
PHOTOGRAPHER NICK GORSKI, NKG STUDIOS
LOCATION NORTHERN WISCONSIN

flanked by high, small windows on each side, the fireplace suggests an *inglenook*, an inviting

and cozy space within a space.

The treatment of wall space in this house incorporates the use of woodwork to lend an

articulated, detailed effect. Throughout the first floor, horizontal bands of trim high on the

wall create the effect of a broad, plain frieze. The door and window framings align with the

frieze. The floors of Brazilian cherry are rich and warm.

To the left of the entry foyer are the kitchen and breakfast area, which open into one

room. The band of trim extends here as well, connecting these more informal rooms to the

rest of the house and continuing the effect of a plain frieze.

PREVIOUS PAGES: *German folk and cottage styles revived in the Arts & Crafts movement—and often characterized by a steeply pitched roof—served as a starting pint for this lake house in northern Wisconsin.*

RIGHT: *A window design suggests the influence of a cottage style. The dense stucco-over-concrete foundation is flared from the base to the start of the clapboard and implies stability, a house rooted to the site.*

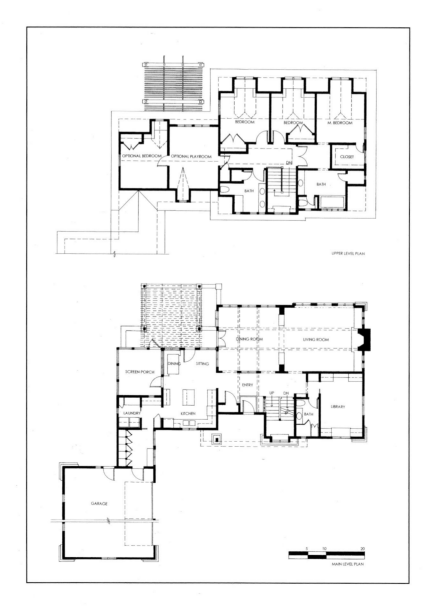

ABOVE: *Arts & Crafts influences are apparent in the entryway. An open screen of spindles extends from the back of a low built-in hall bench.*

ABOVE: *The living and dining rooms open one to another, separated by a low wall. The careful alignment of ceiling beams helps define the space and provides a sense of enclosure. The large fireplace serves as the heart of the house.*

ABOVE: *While painted wood finishes are used throughout most of the house, the library alcove uses a natural finish. The alcove creates a private retreat.*

ABOVE: *The kitchen and breakfast area open into one room.*

RIGHT: *The breakfast alcove.*

ABOVE: *The bathtub sits in a recess.*
Wainscoting lends a sense of detail
and articulation.

ABOVE: *Porch on the back of the house*
with views to the lake.

MARTHA'S VINEYARD HOUSE

Combining Arts & Crafts references with a hipped roof that recalls Japanese forms, this vacation house and garage/guest house sit near a bay on Martha's Vineyard amid forest, marshes, and open farmland. To meet the strict wetlands setbacks and preserve the character of the setting, the main house is long and separated from the garage/guest house. Nonetheless, hipped roofs and arched windows on both suggest a family resemblance despite their differences in plan.

The site is exposed to fierce nor'easters, so the roofs have generous overhangs to protect second-floor ribbon windows. During severe weather, rolling storm doors on the east side of the house may be slid over the more exposed central doors. Cedar shingles on the walls flare at the bottom to direct drips away from the basement walls.

Upstairs and down, three large spaces on each floor connect simply with parallel halls along the exterior walls. On the first floor, a central vaulted space serves as both entryway and formal dining room floored with French limestone. To the right is the kitchen, divided by a high island counter and cabinet; to the left of the entry is the living room with a fossil-stone-faced fireplace. Between these spaces are the powder room, pantry, and skylit stairway.

Upstairs, the ribbon windows offer expansive views across scrub forests and fields to the bay and sea beyond. The windows arch above the building's central entries, front and back. The hallway follows these along the west side, stepping up over the vaulted ceiling below as a bridge to the master bedroom at the end of the house. This suite and the guest bedroom at the other end enjoy windows on three sides, making them feel like open-air pavilions. Over the entry room below is a raised, small study that enjoys the east side's arched window.

ARCHITECT **CENTERBROOK ARCHITECTS AND PLANNERS**
PHOTOGRAPHER **JEFF GOLDBERG/ESTO**
LOCATION **MARTHA'S VINEYARD, MASSACHUSETTS**

Above the garage is a guest room, large and open to a lofty ceilings. Through its arched studio windows, it looks east to the main house across a patch of forest.

PREVIOUS PAGES: *Located on Martha's Vineyard, this house draws on English Arts & Crafts and Japanese references. The hipped roof and dramatic arched windows characterize this island house.*

RIGHT: *Generous roof overhangs protect second-floor windows from the fierce nor'easters that blow in from the sea. Exterior walls covered in cedar shingles flare at the bottom to direct drips away from the basement walls.*

SECOND FLOOR

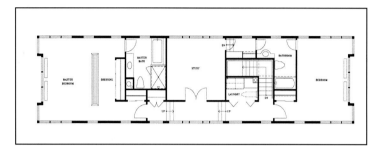

FIRST FLOOR

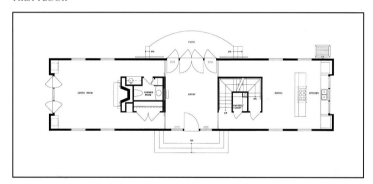

SITE PLAN

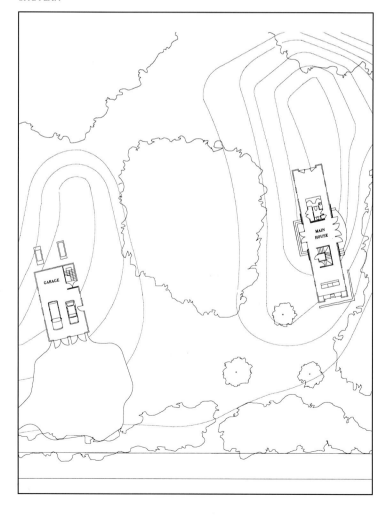

EAST/WEST SECTION

LEFT AND BELOW LEFT: *The garage/guest house, separate from the main house and different in plan, also features a hipped roof and arched windows.*

RIGHT: *The ribbon windows arch above the building's central entries, front and back.*

LEFT: The central vaulted space serves as both entryway and formal dining room.

ABOVE: *The simple fireplace in the living room is faced with fossil stone.*

LEFT: *On the second floor above the entry room, a raised, small study offers a dramatic view through the east side's arched, ribbon window.*

ABOVE: *On the second floor above the entry room, a raised small, study offers a dramatic view through the east side's ribbon window.*

RIGHT: *The upstairs hallway traces along the west side, stepping up over the vaulted ceiling below, which acts as a bridge to the bedrooms at each end of the house.*

FOLLOWING PAGES: *The house sits near a bay on Martha's Vineyard amid forest, marshes, and open farmland.*

CHERRYDALE BUNGALOW

Originally built as a modest two-bedroom, post-World War II brick and block rambler in 1951, this house has assumed an entirely new identity, assimilating the early-twentieth-century Craftsman bungalow aesthetic that makes up most of the Arlington County's Maywood Historic District neighborhood. This house and a twin immediately to the right had for 52 years been the odd houses in a neighborhood of houses developed generations earlier.

The owner had lived in this plain brick box for eight years, making modest changes over time. While these renovations helped to lessen the stark contrast between his house and the Craftsman-style houses in the neighborhood, the changes weren't enough to satisfy the owner's love of the great American bungalow.

The challenge was to create a house that truly fits the neighborhood. The renovated house had to: fit the bungalow style both outside and inside; double the square footage of the existing house, creating new bedrooms on the second floor and reorganizing the first floor spaces; and fit a budget that required the total reuse of the existing structure, including the new replacement windows and new kitchen wing from the owner's earlier renovations.

The existing front wall of the house was pulled forward 3 feet to maximize the existing front yard building setback. A 6-foot-deep porch that stretched across most of the new front elevation was added, pulling the house closer to the street to match the front setbacks of other local early-twentiethth-century houses. This cozier relationship to the street and the public made for a more comfortable, less imposing siting.

The front rooms of the house became new public spaces, with the old living room becoming the inglenook and entry foyer, while the old front bedroom became the new

ARCHITECT **MOORE ARCHITECTS**
PHOTOGRAPHER **HOACHLANDER/DAVIS PHOTOGRAPHY**
LOCATION **ARLINGTON, VIRGINIA**

living room. A new stairway was positioned on axis with the new front door, but set deep into the house adjacent to the reconfigured dining room. The kitchen at the rear that had been opened up during 1996 modifications was closed down again, creating clearly defined spaces, but spaces that are connected visually from room to room.

At the top of the new stair to the second floor is a short, efficient hall with a twin-window view to the rear yard. From this hall are entrances to the master bedroom, second bedroom, and master bathroom. Off of this private space is a study and walk-in closet tucked under the roof eaves of the new second floor.

PREVIOUS PAGES: *The exterior detailing of the house employs reinterpretation of the Craftsman tapered columns and door trim, large overhangs, strong timber outriggers and appropriate wood trim. The house was painted using warm colors that accentuate the different materials and textures.*

SECOND-FLOOR PLAN

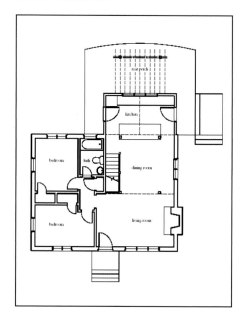

FIRST-FLOOR PLAN

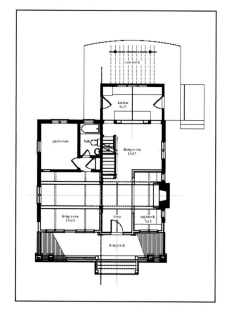

SITE PLAN

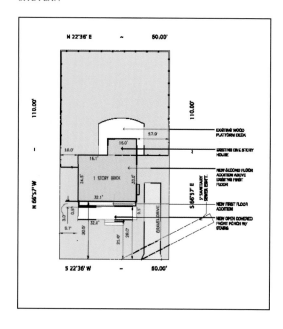

SECTION

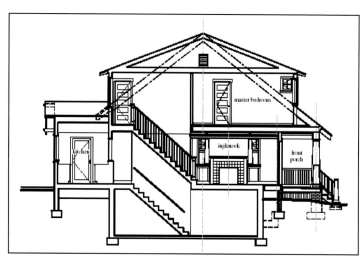

FRONT ELEVATION

REAR ELEVATION

SIDE ELEVATIONS

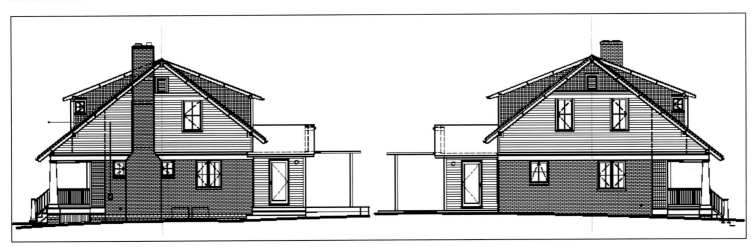

RIGHT: *The existing house before renovations.*

LEFT: *The new stairway was positioned on axis with the new front door. Half walls with tapered columns maintain the open floor plan but define separate spaces.*

RIGHT: *View through interior kitchen window to the entryway and front door. Reproduction tiles are used above the stove.*

LEFT: *An entry foyer and an inglenook with a fireplace were created from the old living room.*

ABOVE: *A view from the dining area to the kitchen. Board and batten style wainscoting adds interest to the dining room.*

INTERIOR ELEVATION DETAILS

ABOVE: *The new master bedroom is located on the centerline of the front of the house. The front dormer, with three exposures of windows, catches the morning light.*

LEFT: *The new master bathroom, adjacent to the master bedroom with an exit to the hall, has matching pedestal sinks with custom wood medicine cabinets, a soaking tub, a large shower with a round-river-stone floor with a high window facing into the rear yard, and wood paneling similar to the new wood paneling on the first-floor spaces.*

RIGHT: *The side gables, rear elevations, and dormers are covered in combinations of cedar shingle and 4-inch exposure lap wood siding.*

FOLLOWING PAGES: *Cherrydale Bungalow at dusk.*

HOLLANDER RESIDENCE

The Hollander Residence is located on 44 acres of rolling countryside with a mix of grasslands and oak, madrone, and fir trees. The house itself sits on a small knoll overlooking a natural swale in the landscape and has distant, layered views of mountains on the horizon. Reflecting Craftsman and Spanish Mission influences, this post and beam, heavy timber house is organized around a south-facing courtyard.

At the core of the house is a flexible common room, which is open to a home office above that occupies the entire second floor. A Tulikivi masonry heater warms the common room and also serves as a cooking oven on the kitchen side of the wall on the south side.

The living room, a place of retreat, is at the end of the house. This area serves as a peninsula of space, with light on three sides. At the end of the room is a nook with a built-in seat that is large enough to serve as a bed, permitting this room to serve as an impromptu guest room. Anchoring the center of the room is a massive stone fireplace on the north side and French doors that step out onto a juliette balcony on the south side.

A thick wall separates the living room from the farmhouse kitchen that is designed as a great room. To that end, all cabinetry is designed as furniture with no traditional upper and lower banks of cabinets. Off to one side, with light on two edges, is a built-in eating nook large enough for six people.

A generous terrace opens off the kitchen and extends across the entire south face of the building. An upper balcony overlooks the terrace from the upstairs home office space. At the far end of the house, the master bedroom is placed in a wing that encloses the terrace on one side.

ARCHITECT JAMES W. GIVENS DESIGN
PHOTOGRAPHER JAMES W. GIVENS
LOCATION EUGENE, OREGON

A stained concrete floor with ground-source heat provides warmth and color throughout the house. Upstairs, Brazilian cherry floors are also warmed by radiant tubing laid beneath it in the joist cavity.

The first-floor master bedroom has an open, relaxed plan. Two special trusses center the room and frame views from the bed the south-facing terrace. An 8-foot-tall wainscot creates the feeling of a room within a room. In the bathroom, the cabinets were designed as furniture. The stone slab has been carved into two shallow bowls for sinks. Nearby, a custom copper tub is nested inside a stone tile surround. The shower is placed as a thick wall between the bathroom and the bed spaces.

The staircase to the second floor is made from thick slabs of fir that form the treads. The office itself is an airy and open plan divided around a large opening to the ground floor. At the far end of the room, a generous rooftop terrace opens to the south.

In every room, the load-bearing timber frame construction is articulated as integral ornament for the house. In the kitchen, two massive braces shoulder a summer beam at the heart of the room. While picking up a large point load from above, it also serves to create an elegant frame to the terrace beyond. In many places, the timber frame is placed and articulated to create a feeling of intimacy.

Port Orford cedar is used on all exterior columns and left to gray naturally with the weather. The exposed structure on the outside of the house—at the front porch, at the back terrace, and at the covered connection from the detached garage and studio to the main house—serves as a preview to the timber frame inside.

PREVIOUS PAGES: *This Craftsman-inspired house–with true post and heavy timber construction–is organized around a south-facing courtyard on 44 acres of rolling countryside with long and layered distant views to mountains on the horizon.*

BOTTOM RIGHT: *Entry façade shows the influence of the Spanish Mission style popular during the Arts & Crafts movement.*

CONCEPT SKETCH

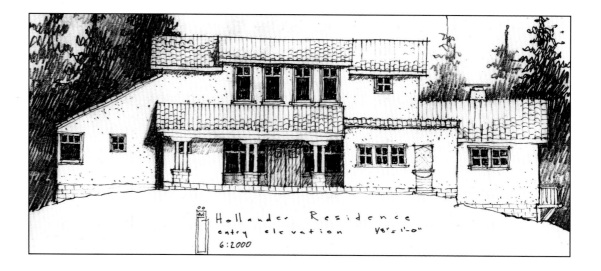

Hollander Residence
entry elevation   1/8"=1'-0"
6:2000

FLOOR PLAN

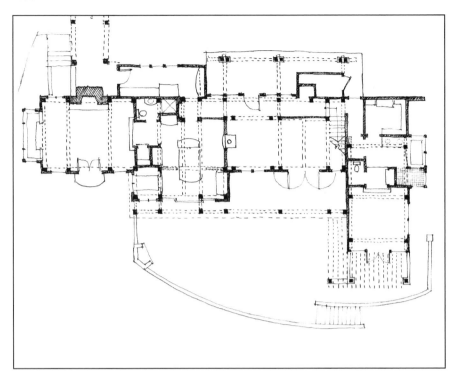

SITE PLAN

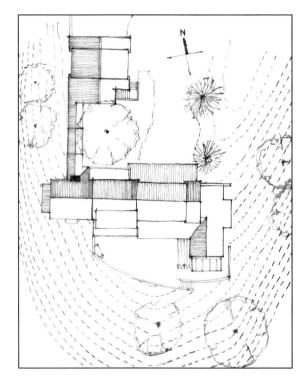

LEFT AND RIGHT: *A library/common room lies at the center of the house and includes a built-in bench and bookshelves. The Tulikivi masonry heater also serves as a cooking oven on the kitchen side of the adjoining wall on the south side. This common room is open to a home office above.*

ABOVE: A second-floor home office occupies the entire floor and looks down into the common room and library below.

RIGHT: The living room, with its massive stone fireplace, is the center of the house. The post and beam construction is both decorative and serves to emphasize the importance of structure and hand craftsmanship. At the end of the room is a window nook with a built-in bench.

ABOVE LEFT: *The farmhouse kitchen serves as a great room. Instead of traditional cabinets with upper and lower banks for storage, the cabinetry is designed as furniture.*

ABOVE: *A kitchen breakfast alcove with light on two sides.*

ABOVE: *Trusses frame the French doors in the kitchen that lead to the courtyard around which the house is organized.*

LEFT: *The first-floor master bedroom opens to the courtyard through French doors. Two special trusses center the room and define an alcove with tall wainscoting that creates the feeling of a cozy room within a room.*

RIGHT: *The bathroom cabinets were designed as furniture. A stone slab was carved into two shallow bowls for sinks.*

DEER ISLE HOUSE

Inspired by the Gamble House in Pasadena, the classic California Arts & Crafts home designed by the architect brothers Greene & Greene, this house is a modified cruciform plan that is also sympathetic to the ecologically sensitive coastal Maine site. Clearing trees from a new house site can open the space to wind and result in the loss of other trees, known as "blow down." Here, efforts were taken to limit clearing and place the house into the landscape.

Drawing on the advice of a forestry consultant, the structure has a modest footprint, but was designed to be as tall as possible with extended overhangs, permitting it to act as a wind spoiler that helps mitigate increased post-construction wind loads on the surrounding trees. To eliminate the need for excavation equipment and lessen the damage to shallow root systems, the building is set on wood poles and concrete piers. Prefabricated stress skin panels and post-and-beam framing were also used allowing the house's shell to be erected with the least amount of on-site construction time possible.

The cross-shaped form inspired by the Gamble House translates into a three-story central spine that accommodates the entrance and kitchen on the first level, an office on the second level, and a belvedere and guest bath on the third level. Flanking the spine on the east side is a two-story wing housing a bedroom, bath, dressing area, and porch on each floor. On the west side of the spine is a two-story great room and screened porch. Dramatically cantilevered decks that thrust seaward create a oneness with the surrounding native spruce trees, just inches away from railings and roof overhangs. Using natural wood and native stone, the interior palette blends with the lofty, open spaces and ample natural light.

ARCHITECT **WINTON SCOTT ARCHITECTS**
PHOTOGRAPHER **BRIAN VANDEN BRINK**
LOCATION **STONINGTON, ME**

THIRD-FLOOR PLAN

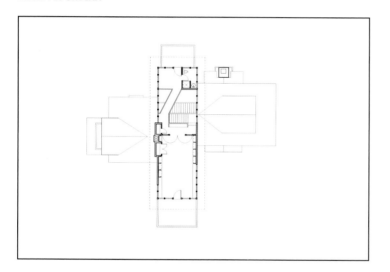

FIRST-FLOOR PLAN

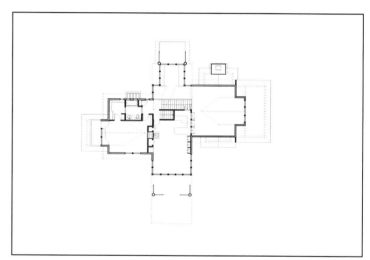

SECOND FLOOR PLAN

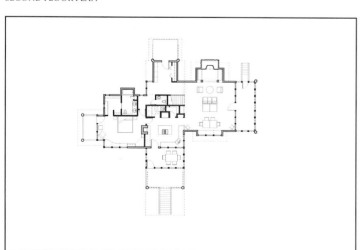

SECTION

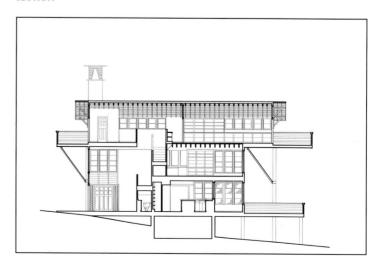

SOUTH ELEVATION

LEFT: *The tree-like Craftsman chimney anchors the house to the site. A cantilevered balcony extended outward from the third level serves as a covered porch over the entrance to the house.*

RIGHT: *Though the house has a modest footprint, it is tall and has extended overhangs. This vertical structure acts as a wind spoiler and helps mitigate wind loads on the surrounding trees. Clearing trees from a new house site often opens the space to wind, resulting in the loss of trees.*

LEFT: *A two-story great room and porch occupy the central wing of the spine.*

RIGHT: *In the great room, the living area is focused around an inglenook, the small recessed "room within a room" by the chimney. Wooden floors and wainscoting tie the spaces together.*

FAR RIGHT: *The three-story central spine has the entrance and kitchen on the first level, an office on the second level, and a belvedere and guest bath on the third level.*

WEST MARY RESIDENCE

An ancient 3-foot-diameter live oak stands guard over this property in one of Austin's older, downtown neighborhoods. Over the years, the tree had grown into the side of a small existing house, which made renovation difficult and preservation of the tree tricky, so after due consideration, the decision was made to carefully dismantle and relocate this structure to a vacant lot nearby. The owner, himself an accomplished woodworker, decided to build a new house that would reflect the style and philosophy of the Arts & Craft period.

With the architect, who also appreciated the work of early California architects, the new house was designed to combine both Craftsman and Asian influences. Austin's hot summer weather encouraged a vernacular response to this style as well. Broad, extended eaves and covered porches shield interior rooms from the daytime sun, and inside, high ceilings permit heat to rise and air to circulate. A fireplace, often a central feature in turn-of-the-century Craftsman homes, was not needed in south Texas.

To accommodate the tree—while at the same time build on a narrow, inner-city lot 50 feet by 136 feet—pier and beam construction was used in sections of the foundation. Piers were placed away from the root system and beams were used to provide maximum width. Inside, the house includes three bedrooms with two and a half baths. Two of the bedrooms are located on the first floor at the rear of the house. The master bedroom is located upstairs with an adjacent study. To take advantage of a panoramic view over the city, a stair tower to a small loft space was added. A garage was built that could double as a wood shop for the owner.

ARCHITECT **JOSEPH M. BENNETT ARCHITECTS**
PHOTOGRAPHER **JACKSON W. SAUNDERS**
LOCATION **AUSTIN, TEXAS**

Stone piers support the wooden beams of the covered porch. On the front porch railing, a "rising cloud" motif is used and is repeated inside on the balcony railing in the study.

PREVIOUS PAGES: *The new house was designed for a narrow, inner-city lot 50 feet by 136 feet that was also home to an ancient live oak tree the owner wanted to preserve.*

SECOND-FLOOR PLAN

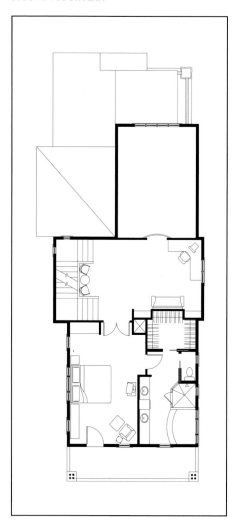

FIRST-FLOOR PLAN

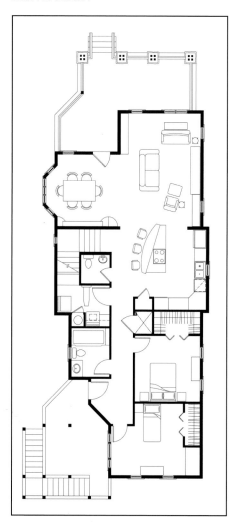

SITE PLAN

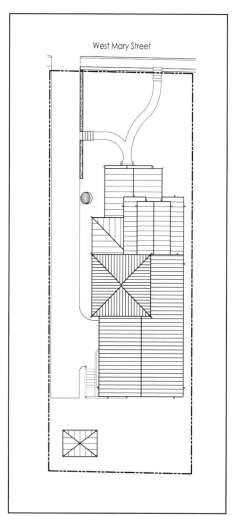

West Mary Street

SECTION

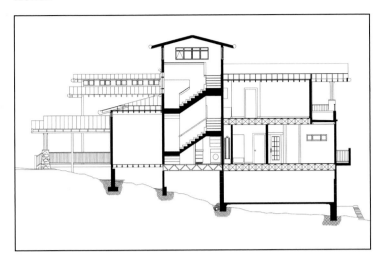

SIDE ELEVATION

FRONT ELEVATION

ABOVE LEFT: *With deep, extended eaves and broad, covered porches, this Craftsman house provides shade during Austin's hot summer weather.*

ABOVE: *High ceilings permit heat to rise and air to circulate in the living room.*

RIGHT: *The kitchen features handcrafted cherry cabinets made by the owner, an accomplished woodworker.*

COUGAR MOUNTAIN

The great rustic National Park lodges and projects built under the WPA program during the 1930s served as a starting point for this house. Mature Douglas firs and hemlocks, as well as a small stream, create a parklike setting on this 1-acre lot east of Seattle on the north face of Cougar Mountain overlooking Lake Sammamish.

The lodge character of the house is Arts & Crafts without being fussy. Outside, the detailing is restrained but bold. The exterior of the house combines cedar shingles and board and batten siding. Split-faced granite columns support roof and decks. Granite walkways and porches and a galvanized metal roof help reduce the maintenance typical with the forest environment.

A local bear visits the property on occasion and has inspired a reoccurring motif found in the light columns that line the driveway, in various handles and knobs in the interior of the house, and in handmade ceramic tiles.

Built also to showcase the owner's collection of Northwest Native American art, the house is built around a great lodge room with vaulted ceilings and exposed timber structures of Douglas fir, reminiscent of those found in a National Park lodge. A stone "water wall" in the entry serves as a background for some of the client's Native American mask collection.

In the lodge room, a massive stone fireplace is faced with split-faced granite; a large beam of recycled Douglas fir serves as the mantel. Douglas fir columns, similar to those that support the roof, support the mantle and are bolted to the granite hearth. Douglas fir paneling is used throughout the room.

The lodge room opens onto the dining room and adjacent kitchen. A laundry and pantry are accessed off a corridor that connects the house by way of a glass bridge

ARCHITECT BAYLIS ARCHITECTS
PHOTOGRAPHER PRO IMAGE PHOTOGRAPHY/ED SOZINHO
LOCATION BELLEVUE, WASHINGTON

to the main garage. This bridge also spans an exterior streambed, which collects and drains storm water away from the front of the house. Also located on the main floor is a guest room with a small private deck accessed through French doors.

The second floor is divided into the master bedroom area and a home office/library. The master bedroom area contains a sleeping room, master bath and walk-in closet, and a small inglenook used as a sleeping/play area with built-in bunks and storage below. The walls are paneled in Douglas fir, lending the room the feeling of a handcrafted wooden boat.

The master bedroom area is connected to the office/library by way of a wooden bridge, which runs above the great room. The office has a stone-faced fireplace and several built-in bookshelves, storage, and is wood paneled throughout. A door opens onto a small outside deck.

PREVIOUS PAGES: *During the 1930s, the WPA built rustic tourist lodges, hotels, and other buildings at many National Parks. These Arts & Crafts-influenced structures inspired the design of this house.*

BELOW: *A rustic stone column marks the entrance to the driveway.*

SITE PLAN

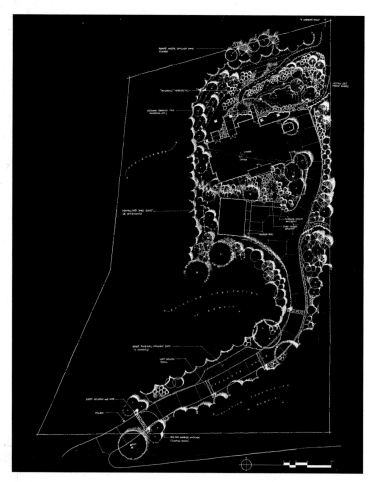

BASEMENT

BASEMENT PLAN (Total Area = 2804sf)

1. GARAGE
2. MECH
3. STORAGE
4. CAR STORAGE
5. STORAGE

FIRST FLOOR

1. GUEST ROOM
2. DECK
3. WALK THRU
4. GUEST BATH
5. POWDER
6. LIVING ROOM
7. ENTRY
8. DINING ROOM
9. DECK
10. BREAKFAST ROOM
11. LAUNDRY
12. PANTRY
13. HALL
14. GARAGE

SECOND FLOOR

OPEN TO
LIVING ROOM
BELOW

OPEN TO ENTRY
BELOW

1. LIBRARY
2. BRIDGE
3. MASTER BED.
4. SITTING
5. MASTER BATH
6. WALK-IN

LEFT: *The house sits amid mature firs and hemlocks on a 1-acre lot on the north face of Cougar Mountain, east of Seattle. A local bear sometimes visits the property.*

BELOW LEFT: *The exterior of the house combines cedar shingles and board and batten siding. Granite piers support roof and decks.*

RIGHT: *Reminiscent of the grand central room found in National Park lodges, the living room has vaulted ceilings and exposed timber structures of Douglas fir. It creates a backdrop for the owner's collection of Northwest Native American art.*

LEFT: *The stone fireplace is faced with split-faced granite; a large beam of recycled Douglas fir serves as the mantel. Douglas fir columns, similar to those that support the roof, support the mantel.*

ABOVE: *Fireplace detail.*

RIGHT: *A stone "water wall" in the entry serves as a background for some of the client's Native American mask collection.*

ABOVE: *The lodge room opens into the dining room and adjacent kitchen.*

LEFT: *The master bathroom.*

ABOVE: *Floor-to-ceiling island with stove in kitchen.*

ABOVE RIGHT: *The master bedroom area is connected to the office/library by way of a wooden bridge, which runs above the great room.*

HOUSE IN CHESTER

Located near the historic town of Chester, this house is surrounded by woodlands that change with the seasons, bringing dappled shade in the summer and filtered light in the winter.

This design goal was to provide the maximum amount of living space within a footprint measuring 30 by 40 feet and incorporate Craftsman-inspired architectural elements and low-maintenance materials, all on a modest budget.

The plan features an open first floor. Beams pinwheel from a central four-sided bookcase pier and serve to differentiate the spaces visually. The use of woodwork, in particular horizontal bands of trim high on the wall, lends an articulated, detailed effect to the treatment of wall space.

The simply detailed, winding three-story staircase ascends on cantilevered intermediate landings. During holidays, the stairs also serve as a continuous stage that wraps the slender 18-foot Christmas tree that is placed at its center.

On the second floor, the hallway widens to become a more livable space and relax the interchange of the bedrooms and stairs. The stairs end at a third-floor master bedroom suite, where storage is provided through a stair-step arrangement of mahogany drawer fronts built into the walls on each side of the room. These "stairs" can be climbed for views out the clerestory windows.

The garage's generous second floor functions as an attic, freeing most of the basement to serve as the wood shop.

A deck on the east side of the house enjoys dappled shade in the afternoon and full shade in the evening. Access is through a door in the dining area.

ARCHITECT **CENTERBROOK ARCHITECTS AND PLANNERS, CHARLES G. MUELLER**
PHOTOGRAPHER **ROBERT BENSON**
LOCATION **CHESTER, CONNECTICUT**

The exterior materials, stucco with vinyl single panels above, were chosen to fulfill the owner's low-maintenance requirements. Used at the second- and third-floor levels, the vinyl shingle panels are convincing and do not turn any outside corners, a condition that typically betrays vinyl siding.

PREVIOUS PAGES: *Incorporating Craftsman-inspired architectural elements both inside and out, this house was designed to provide the maximum amount of living space within a remarkably small footprint and to use low-maintenance materials.*

BASEMENT

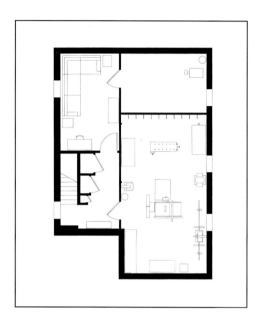

FIRST-FLOOR PLAN

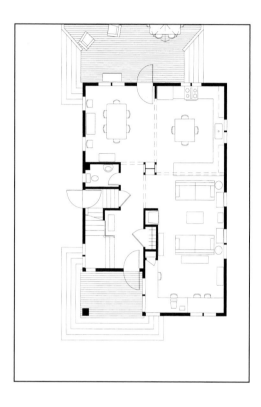

SECOND-FLOOR PLAN

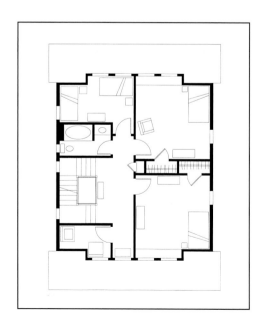

THIRD-FLOOR PLAN

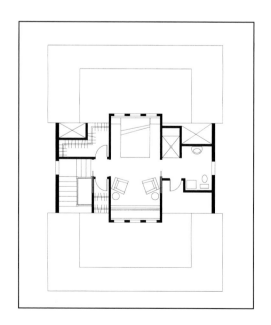

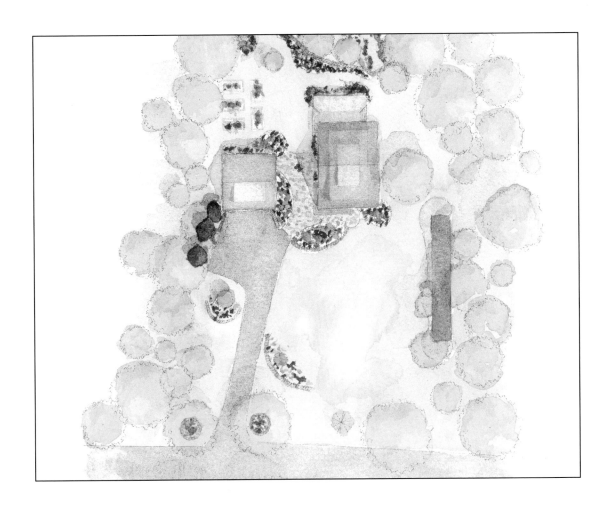

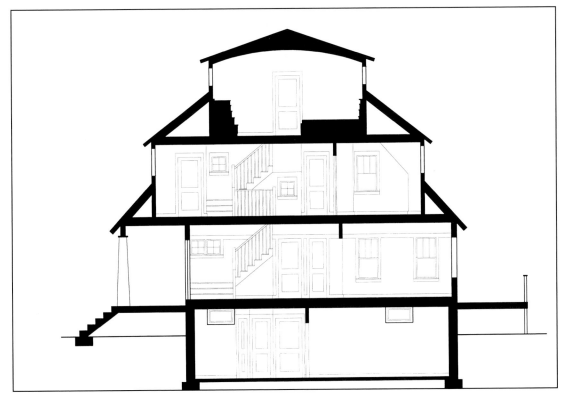

LEFT, BELOW LEFT, AND RIGHT:
The exterior suggests an updated cottage with a steeply pitched roof and broad, horizontal dormers. The front porch with a single tapered column is tucked beneath the eaves. For low maintenance, a combination of stucco and vinyl single panels were used on the exterior.

LEFT: *The simply detailed staircase is the focus of the small entry hall. Four-light windows illuminate the entry and stairwell.*

ABOVE: *The first floor features an open floor plan and conveys a feeling of spaciousness. A four-sided bookcase pier centers the plan. Broad bands of horizontal wood trim extend outward from the bookcase and serve to visually differentiate the kitchen and living and dining areas.*

LEFT: *The kitchen is open to the rest of the first floor.*

ABOVE: *The third-floor master bedroom suite provides storage through a stair-step arrangement of built-in cabinets on each side of the room. These "stairs" can be climbed for views out the clerestory windows.*

BEACH HOUSE

This Beach House on Washington's Bainbridge Island commands a 180-degree view, encompassing a 7-mile reach of open water to the south and an impressive expanse of the Olympic Mountains to the west.

Entering the property at the top of a wooded hill, the driveway curves through landscaping, then down to the house, where intricate rockeries and stone patios and steps envelop the house and connect it with the natural surroundings. A glass-roofed entry, continuous fountain (fed by a curtain drain), and transparent second-floor bridge immediately establish the unique character of this house.

Overlapping the 18-foot-wide footprint of an old beach cabin, just 8 feet from the beach, the new design builds upon the existing foundation's proximity to the water and to the view, and then allows the house to open up beyond current shoreline setbacks. The restricted width, extended 68 feet, inspired a design reminiscent of a pier, stretching out over the water. The long axis is punctuated by glass and culminates in a two-story glass box that takes full advantage of the view. A copper-clad skylight highlights the intersection with the new cross gable.

Double entry doors open to reveal a house filled with exceptional details, contemporary interpretations of Arts & Crafts features and effects. Custom copper lights illuminate fine cabinetry, expert carpentry, and meticulous tile work. Progress through the house is defined by a three-dimensional grid of reclaimed fir posts and beams, ultimately terminating in the living room with windows on three sides.

The exposed site funnels winter storms directly at the house, leading to a selection of natural materials that will patina gracefully. Exterior siding combines yellow cedar shingles and trim with copper panels. A mix of slate and copper cover the roofs.

ARCHITECT J. MACK PEARL
PHOTOGRAPHER MICHAEL MOORE
LOCATION BAINBRIDGE ISLAND, WASHINGTON

SECOND-FLOOR PLAN

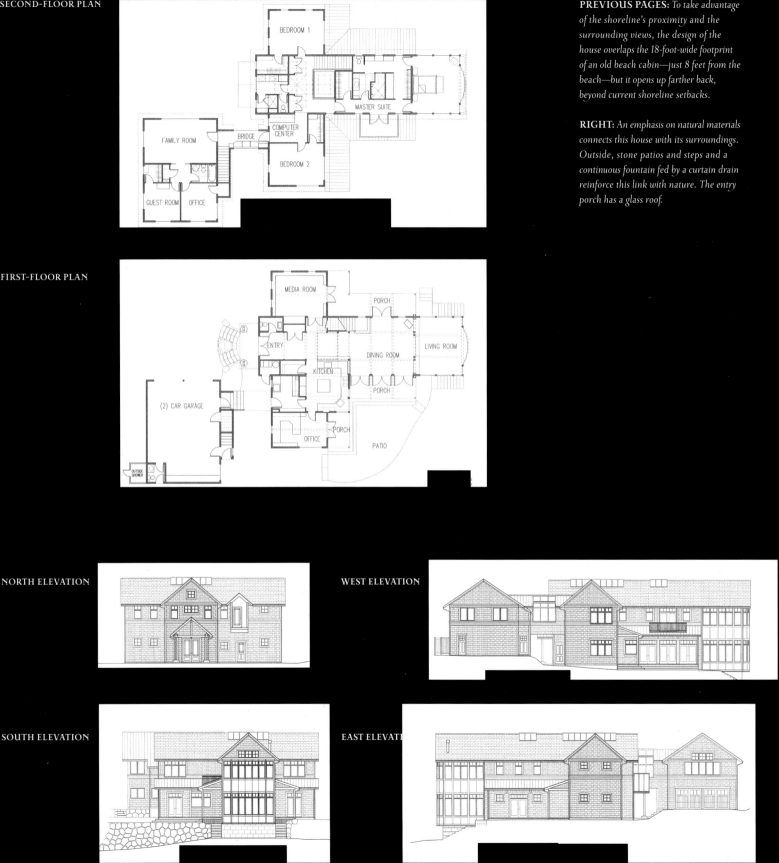

BEDROOM 1

MASTER SUITE

COMPUTER
CENTER

FAMILY ROOM

BRIDGE

BEDROOM 2

GUEST ROOM   OFFICE

FIRST-FLOOR PLAN

MEDIA ROOM

PORCH

ENTRY

DINING ROOM

LIVING ROOM

KITCHEN

PORCH

(2) CAR GARAGE

OFFICE

PORCH

PATIO

OUTSIDE
SHOWER

NORTH ELEVATION

WEST ELEVATION

SOUTH ELEVATION

EAST ELEVATION

PREVIOUS PAGES: *To take advantage of the shoreline's proximity and the surrounding views, the design of the house overlaps the 18-foot-wide footprint of an old beach cabin—just 8 feet from the beach—but it opens up farther back, beyond current shoreline setbacks.*

RIGHT: *An emphasis on natural materials connects this house with its surroundings. Outside, stone patios and steps and a continuous fountain fed by a curtain drain reinforce this link with nature. The entry porch has a glass roof.*

LEFT AND RIGHT: *The design of the house is reminiscent of a pier, stretching out over the water into the vista. The long axis is relieved by glass and culminates in a two-story glass box with windows on three sides.*

LEFT: *Glass-roofed entry with continuous fountain fed by a curtain drain.*

ABOVE AND ABOVE RIGHT: *The entry flows into a center gallery. Inside the house, superb interior construction and fine detailing reflect the Arts & Crafts influence.*

ABOVE LEFT: *Dining area between the kitchen and living room; the alignment of beams and trim helps define the spaces.*

LEFT: *The kitchen*

ABOVE: *The living room overlooking the beach.*

ABOVE LEFT: *Stairway to second floor*

ABOVE: *Second floor*

RIGHT: *Master bedroom*

GORSKI RESIDENCE

Arts & Crafts influences as well as Japanese and vernacular references combine in this Whidbey Island beach house, which looks west across the shipping channel to the Olympic Mountains beyond. To preserve the character of the beach and native vegetation, the house is tucked as far as possible against the wooded slope behind it. In the late afternoon, the setting sun fills the house with bright orange rays.

Deep, 42-inch eaves, braced by wood struts, protect the house from coastal storms. All entries are layered, employing stoops, porches, and sheltered terraces for weather protection.

Rooms are organized around a large central room and are connected visually through the house from front to back. To architect James Givens, this large main room is the Quintessential Room of the house: all movement through the house or to the outside experiences the central room in varying degrees. The room itself is deeply layered: a sleeping alcove glazed on two sides terminates the room; a long L-shaped bench is tucked under a lowered ceiling at the long back of the room; a fireplace anchors the far corner; transom windows with art glass connect the room to the entrance hall and kitchen; massive windows open the center of the room to the beach and to the view. Two concrete columns, in the form of stylized fir trees, form the fireplace and embody the spirit of local imagery and craft. The heart of the room is quietly subdivided by exposed joists above.

Central to the character of this room is the wood used to compose it, cedar boards recycled from a 1920s house that was being dismantled in Oregon. At sunset, as the room begins to glow, the wood assumes a rich, deep tone in the light and releases a subtle, spicy aroma.

ARCHITECT JAMES W. GIVENS DESIGN
PHOTOGRAPHER JAMES W. GIVENS
LOCATION WHIDBEY ISLAND, WASHINGTON

The dining room opens directly to the kitchen and features cedar wainscoting and a cedar ceiling. Interior French doors link to a retreat room for quiet hobbies and reading. Battens and decorative glass belonging to the client were added to standard, flat-panel doors. Access to the beach occurs straight off the dining space via a sheltered stoop.

The upper bedrooms are designed to accommodate numerous guests and visiting families. One bedroom features a cot-sized sleeping bench built into the corner window and at the end of the room, a full-sized sleeping alcove complete with built-in shelving.

PREVIOUS PAGES: *Arts & Crafts influences combined with Japanese and vernacular references are reflected in this beach house on Whidbey Island. With a western exposure, this house enjoys dramatic sunset views across the shipping channel to the Olympic Mountains.*

SECOND-FLOOR PLAN

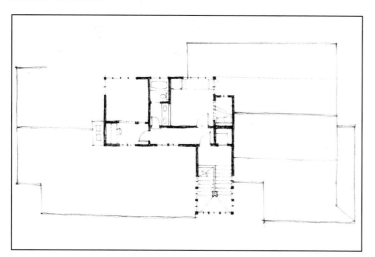

FIRST-FLOOR PLAN

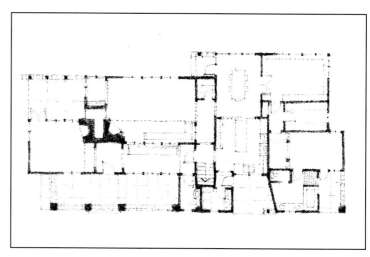

EAST ELEVATION

WEST ELEVATION

SIDE ELEVATIONS

ABOVE: *The house sits away from the shoreline, nestled against the wooded slope behind it in order to preserve the character of the beach and native vegetation.*

LEFT: *Stone piers and paving serve to ground the house and connect it to the landscape.*

ABOVE: *The well-crafted front door is an invitation to enter.*

RIGHT: *Deep, 42-inch eaves, braced by wood struts, protect the house from costal storms.*

ABOVE: *The large main room of the house, the Quintessential Room, is the center of the house, and all circulation through the interior or the exterior experiences this room in varying degrees.*

LEFT: *In the main room, a recess holds a sleeping alcove with windows on two sides.*

ABOVE: *The dining room opens directly to the kitchen and features cedar wainscoting and a cedar ceiling. A door leads to a sheltered stoop and access to the beach.*

RIGHT: *The kitchen.*

PEARSON RESIDENCE

This Craftsman-style house in Oregon rests between a south-facing meadow and a northern grove of oak trees and features deep-sheltering eaves and a large central farmhouse kitchen/hearth room. It is a long, one-room deep plan that terraces gently down the slope of the land.

The ground-floor rooms span from meadow to forest, making the house a threshold between grassy sunlight and the canopied enclosure of trees. Access to the outside happens naturally, at each terrace of the house. Low, shallow roof pitches cascade with the land and create a horizontal reference to the earth. Generous roof overhangs turn into porches, balconies, and trellises that blur the distinction between inside and outside.

The main entrance to the house is modest and low, anchored by the mass of the fireplace nearby. Rooms on the ground floor are linked by a long visual axis that unites the house in a single view.

At the center of the house is the Hearth Room, a tall, broad room that encompasses kitchen, dining, writing, inglenook, and fireplace. Rough-sawn wooden beams, reclaimed from an old bridge, support the room.

The Hearth Room lies at the center of the house, gathering all activity where movement and paths naturally cross. The fireplace becomes an alcove to sit in, just big enough for two. The beam at the joint between the kitchen and the rest of the room is doubled and becomes an ornamental frame. A massive window above the kitchen alcove—measuring over 6 feet in height and 14 feet in width—pulls the northern oak grove up close. At the head of the room is a large, three-sided bay

ARCHITECT JAMES W. GIVENS DESIGN
PHOTOGRAPHER DAVID DUNCAN LIVINGSTON
LOCATION EUGENE, OREGON

window that steps through the perimeter of the house and creates a window place

and culmination to the trellised and terraced edge of the south face of the house.

PREVIOUS PAGES: *Terraced along the slope of the land, this contemporary house is a long, one-room deep plan.*

UPPER-FLOOR PLAN

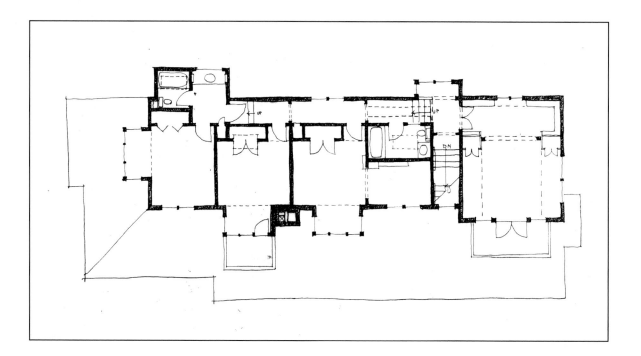

GROUND-FLOOR PLAN

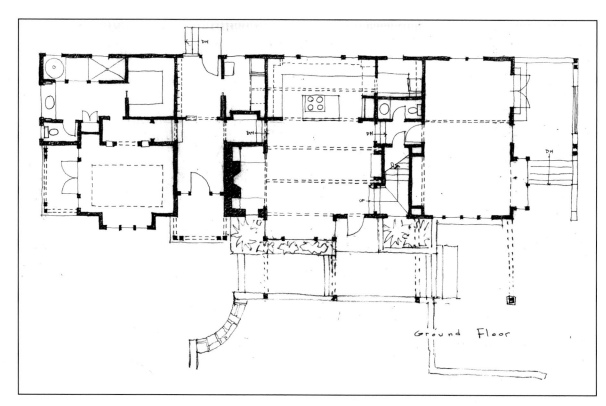

ABOVE AND RIGHT: *Porches, balconies, and trellises blur the distinction between inside and outside.*

ABOVE: *The main entrance to the house is simple and direct. Beamed columns reference Japanese styles and support the roof. The front door shows Craftsman lines and details. The mass of the chimney, inset with art tiles, anchors the entrance.*

ABOVE RIGHT: *Interior view, entry hall.*

RIGHT: *The large, broad Hearth Room at the center of the house encompasses both the kitchen and dining areas, all oriented around a fireplace and an old inglenook.*

FAR RIGHT: *Rough-sawn double beams, reclaimed from an old bridge, frame the kitchen alcove. The large window in the alcove draws the trees inside.*

LEFT: *A library alcove leads into the guest bedroom upstairs. The bookcases and paneled ceiling create an intimate transition from public space to private.*

RIGHT: *View of a bedroom balcony.*

BLOWING ROCK

Built 3,800 feet above sea level in the mountains of western North Carolina, this house responds to the unusually steep topography. The terrain dictated the form, a long, thin house that stretches across the site and stacks vertically over three levels. As a result, each room has breathtaking views across the Blue Ridge Mountains.

For the owners, this house serves as a retirement home and a comfortable gathering place for grown children and many grandchildren. To take advantage of the dramatic vistas, they asked the architect to include a Tower Room as a place to sit quietly and enjoy the uninterrupted views over thousands of acres across Blackberry Gorge, Grandfather Mountain, and Table Rock. The Tower Room also serves to announce the house's presence to visitors and guests. Other special features include a music room, a freestanding elevator, and a porte cochere to shield anyone arriving in bad weather.

While the form of the house is contemporary, the exterior and interior details disclose the owner's enthusiasm for Arts & Crafts influences. Outside are found exposed rafter tails, a post and beam porte cochere, board and batten siding, and cedar shingles. The interior is streamlined, but draws on balanced spaces, and the rich use of natural materials and expressive details.

The color palette throughout the house is subdued and warm. Interior floors are gray-stained oak, and most of the trim is painted. The stairway is vertical-groove oak, and the stair treads are composite cork. The kitchen cabinets are quartersawn white oak.

ARCHITECT **SAMSEL ARCHITECTS**
PHOTOGRAPHER **LAURA MUELLER**
LOCATION **BLOWING ROCK, NORTH CAROLINA**

TOWER PLAN

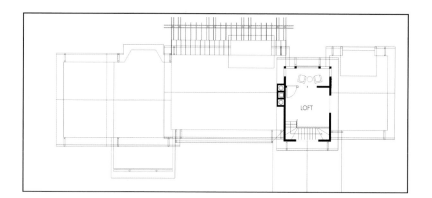

LOFT

PREVIOUS PAGES: *Situated high in the mountains of western North Carolina, this house—inspired by turn-of-the-century Craftsman houses built in the Asheville area—stacks vertically over three levels on a steep site. As a result, each room has breathtaking views over the Blue Ridge Mountains.*

BELOW RIGHT: *The long, thin house responds to a mountain site more than 3,000 feet above sea level.*

MAIN LEVEL

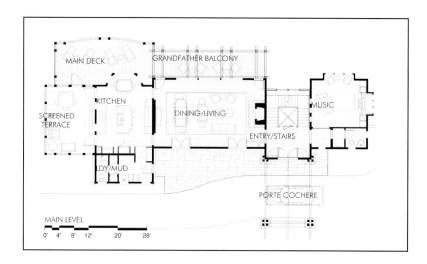

MAIN DECK   GRANDFATHER BALCONY

KITCHEN

SCREENED TERRACE   DINING/LIVING   MUSIC

ENTRY/STAIRS

LDY/MUD

PORTE COCHERE

MAIN LEVEL
0' 4' 8' 12'   20'   28'

LOWER LEVEL

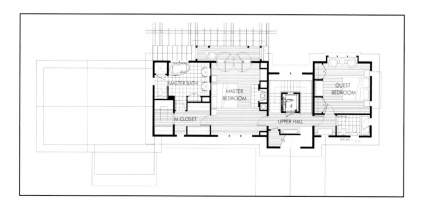

MASTER BATH   MASTER BEDROOM   GUEST BEDROOM

M. CLOSET   UPPER HALL

GROUND LEVEL

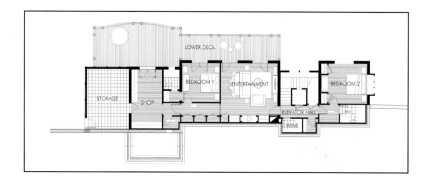

LOWER DECK

BEDROOM 1   ENTERTAINMENT   BEDROOM 2

STORAGE   SHOP

ELEVATOR HALL

WINE

ABOVE: *Fireplace in living room reflects a simple design.*

RIGHT: *The interior is streamlined, but draws on open floor plans and the rich use of natural materials and expressive details typical of the Arts & Crafts style.*

ABOVE LEFT: *The music room is for one of the owners, an accomplished organist.*

ABOVE: *Kitchen with quartersawn oak cabinetry.*

ABOVE: *Master bathroom.*

ABOVE RIGHT: *Bedroom with balcony
and views across the Blue Ridge mountains.*

FOLLOWING PAGES: *Each room has
breathtaking views.*

SECESSIONIST CHALET

Located at Lake Tahoe, the Secessionist Chalet echoes the playful alpine character of this resort. Reminiscent of the Swiss Alps, the surrounding landscape has dramatic mountain peaks and a location that receives more snow than almost anywhere in North America.

The owners wanted a magical winter retreat that would serve as a gathering place for their college-age children and future grandchildren, as well as family friends and world-weary guests. The house was to transport visitors from the uniformity and stress of urban living to the fantasy world of a warm, cozy chalet nestled in the mountains.

The architect looked to the early-twentieth-century Viennese Secessionist architects, in particular Joseph Olbrich, whose work is closely linked to the British Arts & Crafts architects and is often characterized by a rich use of art handicraft. As a result, everything in the house was designed to interpret this style within a contemporary setting. From the knotty alder doors and fine cabinetry to the pierced wood balcony and the Secessionist "rising sun" window, these interior details all work harmoniously to delight the owners and their guests.

On the first floor, an entryway leads into a two-story living room that serves as the heart of the house. The dining room, kitchen, and breakfast room are all positioned to the left of the living room, while a door by the living room fireplace leads into a master bedroom with a private balcony. Upstairs, three bedrooms and an office are situated off the hall. The third floor is a loft space with built-in bunk beds for extra guests.

By incorporating the time-tested materials of copper, stone-fired tile, fritted glass, real masonry, and domestically farmed alder, the chalet demonstrates that simple, enduring materials are remarkable when used in imaginative ways.

ARCHITECT **JOHN MALICK & ASSOCIATES**
PHOTOGRAPHER **JOHN GROVE**
LOCATION **LAKE TAHOE, CALIFORNIA**

GROUND-FLOOR PLAN

PREVIOUS PAGES: *Paying homage to early twentieth-century Viennese Secessionist architecture, this house serves as a retreat—infused with a bit of fantasy—for the owners and their family and friends.*

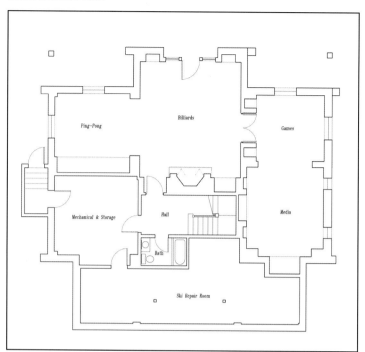

FIRST-FLOOR PLAN

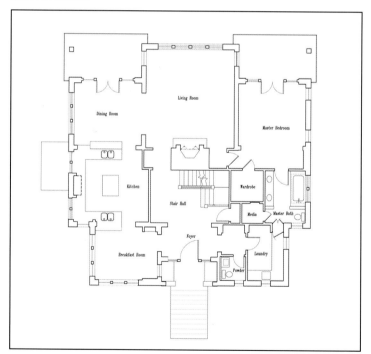

SECOND-FLOOR PLAN

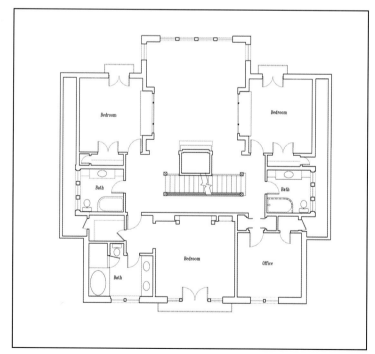

EAST ELEVATION

SOUTH ELEVATION

NORTH ELEVATION

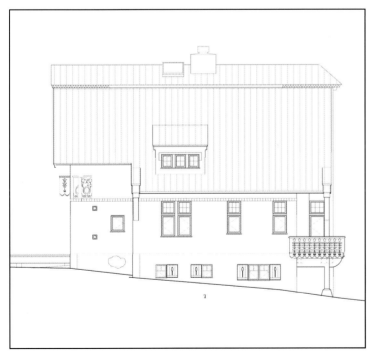

WEST ELEVATION

LEFT: *Reflecting the philosophy of the Arts & Crafts movement, this house is characterized by the rich use of art handicraft inside and out. Everything in the house was designed to interpret this style within a contemporary setting.*

ABOVE: *Balcony detail reflects a folk motif.*

ABOVE: *A Secessionist motif has been adapted for the window in the living room.*

RIGHT: *A two-story living room serves as the heart of the house. An enclosed balcony looks down into the room. The ceiling beams and timber construction are exposed and open to view, reinforcing the craftsmanship and sense of structure.*

LEFT: *The subtly and simplicity of the design is evident in the dining room with its beamed ceiling and knotty alder trim.*

ABOVE: *Kitchen and breakfast room with alder cabinetry and millwork; massive beams frame the breakfast alcove.*

LEFT: *Beamed ceiling in the first-floor master bedroom with doors to balcony.*

ABOVE: *Master bathroom with tile backsplash that draws on a period tile design.*

RIGHT TOP: *Third-floor loft with built-in bunk beds for extra guests.*

RIGHT: *Bunk bed detail.*

FAR RIGHT: *Guest bath with handmade copper sink.*